ROOTED

Daily Devotionals in the Spiritual Disciplines

Kelly Wenner

Rooted: Spiritual Disciplines for Becoming More Like Christ

Written by Kelly Wenner

For permission requests, contact:
Kelly Wenner
www.kellywenner.com

ISBN: 979-8-9929143-7-5

Table of Contents

Welcome to ROOTED

Welcome to ROOTED

Welcome to Rooted:

Spiritual Disciplines for Becoming More Like Christ

For many of us, faith is something we *want* to grow in… but the pace of life makes it hard to slow down, focus, and actually walk with intention. We long to feel closer to the Lord, but our days are filled with distractions, responsibilities, and constant hurry.

The truth is this: deep spiritual growth rarely happens by accident. It happens through small, steady habits—through simple choices that help us draw near to God in the middle of real life.

Spiritual Disciplines: Becoming More Like Christ is a six-week devotional designed to help you build those habits with purpose and clarity. Throughout this journey, you'll explore practices that Christians have used for centuries to cultivate a faithful, steadfast life—practices like meditating on Scripture, prayer, confession, stillness, humility, service, and learning to live each day for Christ.

This devotional isn't about perfection or pressure. It's not about doing more or checking spiritual tasks off a list. It's about creating space for God to shape you—one small, practical step at a time.

Over the next six weeks, you will:

- Slow down enough to hear God's voice through His Word
- Examine the habits that shape your heart and daily decisions
- Learn to pray with honesty, humility, and trust
- Practice confession and surrender
- Develop spiritual self-discipline
- Grow in Christlike love, compassion, and service
- Discover what it means to live every day "in the name of Jesus"

Each day includes Scripture, reflection, and an action step that helps you live out what you're learning—not just read about it. Whether you're beginning this journey on your own or walking through it with a small group, these pages will guide you toward intentional habits that nurture your spiritual growth and strengthen your relationship with the Lord.

Pairing This Devotional with SoulStrength Fit

If you'd like to deepen this experience further, Spiritual Disciplines pairs seamlessly with the SoulStrength Fit program, which includes at-home strength training workouts that directly correspond with each week's devotionals. These workouts help you strengthen your body while drawing near to the Lord, turning your time spent exercising into a meaningful way to honor your temple. It's a simple way to bring your time with the Lord into your exercise routine, strengthening both body and spirit in a focused, faith-centered way. You can learn more at www.soulstrengthfit.com.

Welcome to ROOTED

As you begin this devotional, remember this:
God meets you in the small things. In the moments of quiet. In the honest prayers. In the Scriptures that speak to you at just the right time. In the simple habits that slowly reshape your heart.

My prayer is that this journey helps you grow closer to Him, develop life-giving disciplines, and experience the joy, peace, and strength that come from walking with Christ daily.

Let's begin this six-week journey together—learning to slow down, refocus, and build a life anchored in God's truth and presence.

Week 1

Meditating on Scripture

Day 1: Are You Double-Minded?

Read: James 1:4–8

What does it mean to be "double-minded"? Where does this tendency come from, and how does it affect your spiritual growth?

What would you say are three primary reasons to read the Bible?

Currently, how do you feel about the time you dedicate to reading and meditating on Scripture? Are there any changes you'd like to make? What might those look like?

Jesus calls His followers to seek one thing: His kingdom and His righteousness above all else. When we center our lives on Him—when knowing Him, loving Him, and walking in His ways becomes our primary pursuit—it changes everything. Our thoughts, words, and actions begin to reflect a unified purpose.

But let's be honest: most of us struggle with divided loyalties. We want to seek the Lord, but the constant demands of daily life—our schedules, errands, and responsibilities—often steal our focus. Though we long to live faithfully, we often find ourselves doing the opposite.

Read: Romans 7:14–25

Can you relate to the struggle Paul describes—wanting to do good, but struggling to carry it out? In what situations is this struggle the greatest for you?

Now consider Paul's conclusion to this struggle:
"Thanks be to God, who delivers me through Jesus Christ our Lord!"

Thanks be to God, indeed!

Close your time with this reading:

Read: Ephesians 2:1–12

Ask the Lord to help you focus your heart and mind on Him alone, confessing your tendency toward double-mindedness and asking for the strength to seek Him first.

Action Step:

Choose one verse from today's reading and meditate on it throughout your day. Write it on a sticky note, save it as your phone background, or repeat it during quiet moments.

Day 2: Jesus Has Called You as a Disciple

In Jesus' day, religious teachers—called rabbis—would invite followers, or disciples, to learn from them and follow in their footsteps. A disciple of Jesus is simply someone who has chosen to follow Him. This was the very command Jesus gave to His first disciples: "Follow me."

Read: Matthew 4:18–25

As Disciples of Christ, we are learning to root our identity in Him. Our aim is to become more and more like Jesus as we intentionally walk in His ways.

"Students are not greater than their teacher. But the student who is fully trained will become like the teacher."
Luke 6:40

In what ways are you currently living out your walk as a disciple of Jesus? In what ways would you like to grow as one of Christ's disciples?

Read the following verses that describe your identity in Christ:

You are God's child.

"See how very much our Father loves us, for he calls us his children, and that is what we are! But the people who belong to this world don't recognize that we are God's children because they don't know him."
1 John 3:1

You are a foreigner in this world.

"Dear friends, I warn you as 'temporary residents and foreigners' to keep away from worldly desires that wage war against your very souls."
1 Peter 2:11

You are an ambassador for Christ.

"This means that anyone who belongs to Christ has become a new person. The old life is gone; a new life has begun!... So we are Christ's ambassadors; God is making his appeal through us. We speak for Christ when we plead, 'Come back to God!'"
2 Corinthians 5:17, 20

How do you respond to these truths about who you are in Christ—that you are God's child, a foreigner in this world, and an ambassador for Christ?

Which identity do you find most challenging to live out? Why?

Close your time with prayer.

Thank God for the calling to be His disciple. Praise Him for His presence and goodness in your life. Ask for wisdom and growth as you follow Him more closely.

Action Step:

Make a list of 3–5 specific ways you can grow as an ambassador for Christ this week. Consider areas such as how you spend your time, your mindset, thoughts, and attitude, and the extent to which the fruit of the Spirit is evident in your daily life. Pray over this list and ask God to reveal where He wants to grow and shape you as His ambassador.

Day 3: Growing in Self-Control

Read: Hebrews 4:12–13

What do you think it means that God's word is "alive and active"?

This verse uses the image of a sword to describe the power of Scripture—sharp, precise, and penetrating. Like a surgeon's scalpel, God's word exposes what's beneath the surface, cuts away what's infected, and works to bring healing and transformation. It reaches the places in us that no one else can reach, reshaping our hearts to look more like Christ.

What area of your life might currently need the penetrating and transforming power of God's word? Where might God want to make you more like Jesus?

Read: Titus 2:11–14

What does this passage say the grace of God teaches us to do?

In what areas of your life do you need help with self-control? Where do you need help saying "no" to ungodliness?

Close your time with this reading:
Read: Psalm 119:1–17

Ask God to give you a heart that is teachable, humble, and responsive to His Word. Invite Him to strengthen your self-control and help you walk in obedience.

Action Step:

Identify one area where you've been struggling with self-control—whether in thought, attitude, or action. Find a verse from today's reading that speaks to that area, and write it somewhere you'll see it often this week. Let that verse be your reminder and your weapon as you choose to live by God's grace.

Day 4: Are You Sharing the Good News?

Read: John 1:29–42

What does this passage teach you about Jesus? Which parts of John's description point to the truth that Jesus is fully God and fully human? (See verses 30–34)

What portions of John's description highlight Jesus' mission and purpose on earth? (See verse 29)

To be a disciple of Christ, we must first understand who He is and why He came. But true discipleship goes beyond comprehension—it requires participation. To follow Jesus is to join in His mission here on earth.

John the Baptist took action by publicly proclaiming Jesus' identity. Andrew responded by immediately telling his brother, Simon, about the Messiah he had found.

What has been your experience with talking to others about Jesus?

In addition to sharing the gospel directly, what are some other ways you can participate in Jesus' mission to the world?

Read: Luke 3:15–17

"Everyone was expecting the Messiah to come soon, and they were eager to know whether John might be the Messiah. John answered their questions by saying, 'I baptize you with water; but someone is coming soon who is greater than I am—so much greater that I'm not even worthy to be his slave and untie the straps of his sandals. He will baptize you with the

Holy Spirit and with fire. He is ready to separate the chaff from the wheat with his winnowing fork. Then he will clean up the threshing area, gathering the wheat into his barn but burning the chaff with never-ending fire.'"

What do you learn about John the Baptist from these verses?

What do you learn about Jesus from these verses?

We are disciples of Christ. We join with one another—and with disciples around the world—to participate in the mission of Jesus: the One "who takes away the sin of the world." To be His disciple is to seek Him, serve Him, and share Him with others.

Close your time in prayer.

Talk with the Lord about how He may want to use you as His loved and chosen disciple. Ask Him to give you both the heart and the boldness to participate in His mission.

Action Step:

Identify one way you can participate in Jesus' mission this week—whether it's through a conversation, an act of service, or intentional prayer for someone who needs Christ. Write it down, pray over it, and follow through.

"Go where your best prayers take you."
— Frederick Buechner

Day 5: Lord, Open Our Eyes

Read: 2 Timothy 3:14–17

According to these verses, how is Scripture useful? Now personalize this passage. What might teaching, rebuking, correcting, and training in righteousness look like in your life? What good works might God be equipping you to do?

Read: Luke 24:13–35

To meditate on Scripture means to slow down, reflect, and ask the Holy Spirit to guide your understanding—just as Jesus did with the disciples on the road to Emmaus.

"Then their eyes were opened and they recognized him."

Sometimes we need help understanding Scripture. Sometimes we need help with our faith. Sometimes we need help seeing Jesus at work in our lives.

Where do you need your eyes to be opened? How might you pray for the Holy Spirit to increase your understanding and strengthen your faith?

After their eyes were opened, what did the disciples do in response?

When you encounter Christ—when you come to know Him, understand who He is, and experience His love—you take action.

"Do not merely listen to the word, and so deceive yourselves. Do what it says. Anyone who listens to the word but does not do what it says is like someone who looks at his face in a mirror and, after looking at himself, goes away and immediately forgets what he looks like. But whoever looks intently into the perfect law that gives freedom, and

continues in it—not forgetting what they have heard, but doing it—
they will be blessed in what they do."
James 1:22–25

Internalizing, memorizing, and meditating on Scripture will deepen your walk with God in powerful ways. Studying the Bible will give you a clearer understanding of God's character and truth than anything else. When you slow down to reflect on Scripture, you begin to notice details and insights you would have missed by simply reading quickly through a passage.

It's like the difference between driving through your neighborhood and taking a slow walk through it. Driving shows you the big picture—but walking helps you appreciate every flower, tree, and detail along the way. The goal is not to simply *get through* scripture; the goal is to allow scripture to *get through to you.*

"Trust in the Lord with all your heart
and lean not on your own understanding;
in all your ways submit to him,
and he will make your paths straight."
Proverbs 3:5–6

When God's Word is hidden in your heart, you are equipped to walk any path. You don't have to rely on your own understanding—you have God's grace and wisdom to guide you. Scripture provides the clarity you need to make wise decisions, and the peace you need in the face of anxiety or confusion.

"Finally, brothers and sisters, whatever is true, whatever is noble, whatever is right, whatever is pure, whatever is lovely, whatever is admirable—if anything is excellent or praiseworthy—think about such things."
Philippians 4:8

Meditating on and memorizing Scripture fills your heart and mind with what is excellent and praiseworthy. When you feel overwhelmed, anchoring your thoughts in God's truth will strengthen and comfort you like nothing else.

Close your time in prayer.

Ask the Lord to open your eyes, increase your understanding, and help you stay rooted in His Word. Invite Him to guide you daily and equip you for the good works He's calling you to do.

Action Step:

Make a commitment today. Decide how often and how long you will spend in Scripture each week—and write it down. Let this be a joyful priority in your life.

I will commit to _______ days per week to read my Bible, meditate on Scripture, or memorize Bible verses. Time of day I will do this: _______________________
Amount of time I will spend daily: _________________

Remember:

God is faithful. He who began a good work in you will be faithful to complete it. He wants to know you, speak to you, and walk with you—and time in His Word is one of the most powerful ways to respond to that invitation.

Week 2

Practice Slowing Down & Celebrating

Day 1: You Can't Follow Jesus in a Rush

It's critical to realize that we cannot follow Jesus in a hurry. We can't think as He thinks, love as He loves, or act as He would act when we're constantly rushing. Hurry keeps our minds fixed on problems and distractions, and it prevents Jesus' perspective from settling in our hearts.

Hurry keeps us from *living* to our fullest and *loving* to our fullest. It drains our joy, makes us less patient and loving, and hinders our spiritual growth. Think of hurry as a subtle but serious enemy to your walk with God. You can't move faster than the One you're following—so if you want to follow Jesus, you must regularly slow down enough to actually stay in step with Him.

When are you most prone to letting hurry keep you from following Jesus? When does rushing prevent you from experiencing His peace or seeing things through His perspective?

How many times a day do thoughts like "I don't have time," "I'm so behind," or "I have too much to do" run through your mind?

What are the main reasons you find yourself constantly rushing?

Jesus was often busy, but never hurried. He regularly stepped away to nurture His relationship with the Father, so that His life fully aligned with His Father's will. When we slow down and make time for solitude, we retreat from the noise of the world so we can reconnect with the presence of God.

Read: Mark 6:30–46

Notice an ordinary day in the life of Jesus. What stands out to you about His actions and choices?

Jesus had a full and demanding day. How do you tend to handle busy days? How do they affect your mood, your reactions, or your ability to love and care for others?

Read: Luke 5:12–16

Even though people constantly needed Jesus' attention, what did He choose to do at the end of the passage?

How would it impact your spiritual life to find small moments of solitude, even in the middle of your busiest days? How might regular moments of quiet and prayer help you reconnect with God?

How would this rhythm of stillness also benefit your relationships? Who in your life might be blessed when you slow down, center yourself in God's peace, and respond with more love, patience, or presence?

Close your time today in stillness before God.

Read: Psalm 46:1–10

Take a few unhurried moments to be still and know that He is God. Ask Him to help you make space for His presence in the midst of your day.

Action Step:

Identify one moment in your daily routine where you can build in solitude—a five-minute pause before the day begins, a walk without distractions, or a quiet space for prayer before bed. Write down when and where you'll do this, and commit to protecting that time with God.

Day 2: Disciples of Christ

Read: Matthew 28:18–20

"Jesus came and told his disciples, 'I have been given all authority in heaven and on earth. Therefore, go and make disciples of all the nations, baptizing them in the name of the Father and the Son and the Holy Spirit. Teach these new disciples to obey all the commands I have given you. And be sure of this: I am with you always, even to the end of the age.'"

This passage is commonly known as The Great Commission.

How might the action words *go*, *baptizing*, and *teaching* be lived out in your current circumstances? How can you personally apply this Great Commission to your life—right now—with the relationships, responsibilities, and places God has entrusted to you?

Now put this moment in context. Reread Matthew 28 in its entirety.

What key events occurred just before Jesus gave this command? How might those events have shaped the disciples' understanding of what He was asking them to do?

It's important to recognize that Jesus' mission flows directly from His divine identity and authority. He can heal what is broken because He created it. He can forgive sins because He is holy, sinless, and fully God. Living as disciples of Christ means embracing this truth with our whole lives.

"My sheep listen to my voice; I know them, and they follow me. I give them eternal life, and they will never perish. No one can snatch them away from me, for my Father has given them to me, and he is more powerful than anyone else. No one can snatch them from the Father's hand. The Father and I are one." John 10:27–30

Jesus was clear about His identity—and just as clear about His mission.

"Whoever wants to be a leader among you must be your servant, and whoever wants to be first among you must be the slave of everyone else. For even the Son of Man came not to be served but to serve others and to give his life as a ransom for many." Mark 10:43–45

How does this impact the way you view your role as a disciple?

"After saying all these things, Jesus looked up to heaven and said, 'Father, the hour has come. Glorify your Son so he can give glory back to you. For you have given him authority over everyone. He gives eternal life to each one you have given him. And this is the way to have eternal life—to know you, the only true God, and Jesus Christ, the one you sent to earth. I brought glory to you here on earth by completing the work you gave me to do. Now, Father, bring me into the glory we shared before the world began.'" John 17:1–5

Reflect on this: Paul once wrote, *"I urge you to imitate me."* (1 Corinthians 4:16)

Could you imagine saying that to the people in your life? Why or why not?

What would need to change for you to confidently invite others to imitate your faith?

Close your time in prayer.

Ask the Lord to deepen your understanding of what it means to be His disciple. Pray for the humility to follow and the boldness to share His truth in your everyday life.

Action Step:

Think of one person in your life who needs to see or hear the love of Christ through you. Write down one way you can be a disciple-maker this week—whether through encouragement, service, prayer, or conversation.

Day 3: Slow Down

Read: Luke 10:38–42

How did Jesus view this situation between Mary and Martha? Mary is a beautiful example of undistracted devotion to God. We don't want God pushed to the edges of our focus—we want Him at the center. Even though Mary faced many of the same distractions you and I do—like the pressure of tasks and responsibilities—she chose what mattered most. She stopped. She listened. She focused on Jesus.

But how can we do this consistently in our day-to-day lives? How can we fix our eyes on Christ when everything around us feels urgent, chaotic, or overwhelming?

Sometimes it's in those very moments—when the pressure is rising and your energy is fading—that you need to pause and simply whisper a short prayer:

"God, be with me."
"God, give me the strength I need."
"God, help me to slow down and sense Your presence."

Think back over the past few days or the past week. When were the moments you would have benefited from stopping? Were there times when slowing down—even briefly—might have protected your peace, helped you avoid anxious thoughts, or changed the way you responded?

What situations would have looked different if you had taken a moment to pause and turn to the Lord?

To eliminate hurry doesn't simply mean checking more items off your to-do list. It means reordering your life and your heart. Scripture warns us repeatedly about the distractions and false priorities that pull us away from God:

Chasing wealth.
Seeking approval.
Building an image.
Pursuing recognition or power.
Worrying about material needs.
Living for comfort and pleasure.

When these things take first place, our lives become hurried and heavy.

Which of these worldly pursuits tends to distract you the most? Which ones contribute to a sense of constant rushing or restlessness in your life?

Read: Matthew 6:19–34

According to Jesus, what does it look like to properly "order" your heart?

Close your time in prayer.

Ask God to help you notice the moments when you need to slow down and turn to Him. Invite Him to help you reorder your heart and live with greater focus and peace.

Action Step:

Choose one moment today when you'll practice the discipline of slowing down. When that moment comes, pause—breathe, pray, and turn your attention to God. Whether it's before a task, a conversation, or a moment of stress, let it be an intentional act of choosing the "better part."

Day 4: You Have Been Called

Read: Luke 10:1–23

What power and authority did Jesus give to His disciples? As a disciple of Christ today, what power and authority do you believe you've been given?

How are you currently using—or neglecting—those spiritual gifts and responsibilities?

"When the apostles returned, they reported to Jesus what they had done. Then he took them with him and they withdrew by themselves to a town called Bethsaida." Luke 9:10

What role did Jesus play after the disciples returned from their mission?

In what ways does Jesus play a similar role in your life today?

Jesus calls His disciples.
Jesus teaches His disciples.
Jesus equips His disciples.
Jesus sends His disciples.

Now take a moment to personalize these truths:

I have been called by Jesus to:

At this point in my spiritual journey, I have been taught these truths:

I have been equipped with (talents, skills, personality traits, or resources):

I believe Jesus is sending me to (a person, group, or mission):

Being a disciple of Christ is not a casual role or something we squeeze into the margins of our lives. It's not like joining a club or volunteering when we have time. It's a calling that shapes how we live, who we love, and how we spend our days.

"Then he said to the crowd, 'If any of you wants to be my follower, you must give up your own way, take up your cross daily, and follow me. If you try to hang on to your life, you will lose it. But if you give up your life for my sake, you will save it.'" Luke 9:23–24

Close your time in prayer.

Sit in stillness before the Lord. Ask Him to speak to you clearly—about your calling, your readiness, and the next step He's asking you to take as His disciple.

Action Step:

Choose one area from today's reflection—something you've been called to, taught, equipped for, or sent into—and write down a small step of obedience you can take this week. Ask God for the courage and clarity to follow through.

Day 5: Are You a Joyful Person?

G.K. Chesterton once wrote:

> *"It is possible that God says every morning, 'Do it again' to the sun; and every evening, 'Do it again' to the moon. It may not be an automatic necessity that makes all daisies alike; it may be that God makes every daisy separately but has never got tired of making them. It may be that He has the eternal appetite of infancy; for we have sinned and grown old, and our Father is younger than we."*

Do you picture God as joyful? Do you imagine Him creating the world with delight? Can you see Him finding joy in the rising and setting of the sun, in the beauty of nature, and in knowing and loving each of His children—including you?

Let's go back to the very beginning.

Read: Genesis 1:1–31

Again and again we read, "*God said… And it was so.*" *And again and again we read,* "And God saw that it was good."

Do you find joy in the rhythms of creation—the rising sun, the beauty of trees and skies, the people around you, or the unique person God made you to be?

Take a moment to reflect with gratitude. Every good and perfect gift is from above. God wants you to find joy in His gifts and to experience His joy in your life.

List a few things, people, or experiences you are grateful for today:

"But the fruit of the Spirit is love, joy, peace, patience, kindness, goodness, faithfulness, gentleness and self-control. Against such things there is no law. Those who belong to Christ Jesus have crucified the flesh with its passions and desires." Galatians 5:22–24

Joy is a fruit of the Spirit—the Spirit of God. When you walk by the Spirit, you reflect the character of God. When you express joy, you are imitating Him.

Be honest—on a scale of 1–10, how joyful would you say you are?

Would others describe you as joyful?

What tends to steal your joy most often? Is it worry, stress, hurry, comparison, envy, or a lack of gratitude?

Conclude your time with these verses:

John 15:9–11 (NIV):

"As the Father has loved me, so have I loved you. Now remain in my love. If you keep my commands, you will remain in my love, just as I have kept my Father's commands and remain in his love. I have told you this so that my joy may be in you and that your joy may be complete."

Philippians 4:4–7 (NIV):

"Rejoice in the Lord always. I will say it again: Rejoice! Let your gentleness be evident to all. The Lord is near. Do not be anxious about anything, but in every situation, by prayer and petition, with thanksgiving, present your requests to God. And the peace of God, which transcends all understanding, will guard your hearts and your minds in Christ Jesus."

1 Thessalonians 5:16–18 (NIV):
"Rejoice always, pray continually, give thanks in all circumstances; for this is God's will for you in Christ Jesus."

Close your time in prayer.

Ask God to restore a sense of joy in your heart today. Thank Him for His gifts, His Spirit, and His presence. Invite Him to help you reflect His joy to those around you.

Action Step:

Choose one way to express joy intentionally today—through gratitude, encouragement, or simply delighting in a part of creation. Make a conscious decision to reflect the joy of the Lord in your attitude and actions.

Week 3

Prayer & Confession

Day 1: Come Now to Jesus in Prayer

Many people feel that their prayer life isn't what it should be. Often, we turn to prayer when something goes wrong—when we feel desperate, overwhelmed, or out of control. In those moments, prayer flows more easily. But in the normal, everyday moments of life, prayer can feel like an afterthought.

Why do you think that is? Why don't we pray more often or more consistently?

Begin your time today by praying. Use these prompts as a guide to draw your heart into communion with God:

- Acknowledge that God alone is worthy of worship, honor, praise, and adoration.
- Thank Him for inviting you—an imperfect person—into a relationship with a perfect and loving God.
- Confess anything pulling your attention away and ask God to remove all distractions during this time.
- Thank Him for every good and perfect gift in your life.

There are many reasons we may neglect prayer. We often trust ourselves more than God and try to maintain control that was never ours to begin with. Sometimes we doubt whether our prayers really matter—or if they're even heard. Other times, we're simply too distracted to remember we've been invited into a limitless, personal conversation with the God of the universe.

Whatever the reason, we often miss out on the joy and power of prayer. But God is always waiting—inviting you to draw near.

Jeremiah 29:11–13

"For I know the plans I have for you," declares the Lord, "plans to prosper you and not to harm you, plans to give you hope and a future. Then you will call on me and come and pray to me, and I will listen to you. You will seek me and find me when you seek me with all your heart."

For I know the plans I have for you," declares the Lord, "plans to prosper you and not to harm you, plans to give you hope and a future. Then you will ______ on me and come and ________________, and I will __________________. You will seek me and _______________when you seek me with all your heart.

Throughout Scripture, Jesus modeled a life of prayer. One of the clearest examples is the prayer He taught His disciples.

Read: Matthew 6:5–13

What differences do you notice between verses 5–8 and verses 9–13?
Which part of this prayer speaks most deeply to you right now? Why?

Today, invite God to walk with you throughout your day. Bring prayer into all the ordinary moments—while driving, cooking, folding laundry, working, or caring for your family. Prayer doesn't need to be reserved for morning quiet time or bedtime routines. It can be a constant, living conversation.

Close your time in prayer.

Thank God for the invitation to walk with Him in every moment. Ask Him to deepen your desire for prayer and to help you become aware of His presence throughout your day.

Action Step:

Choose three everyday activities today—such as driving, eating, or doing chores—and intentionally turn them into moments of prayer. Practice inviting God into the ordinary, and begin building a habit of ongoing connection.

Day 2: Are You Willing to Take Up Your Cross?

Read: Luke 9:18–27

What are the conditions and promises Jesus lays out for those who want to follow Him?

What do you believe it means to *deny yourself* and *take up your cross*?
Give a few examples of how this might look in your everyday life—relationships, decisions, thought patterns, or priorities.

How might someone attempt to "save" their own life in the way Jesus warns about?

What are some ways you've experienced this in your own life—clinging to control, striving for comfort, or pursuing self-made security?

Jesus wasn't necessarily talking about physically dying for His mission (though many believers throughout history have). What He wants us to understand is that being His disciple means surrendering our lives to Him. It means trusting Him with our future, submitting to His leadership, and releasing our grip on our plans.

Being a disciple of Jesus isn't just about believing He is our Savior—it's about surrendering to Him as our Lord and King.

In what ways have you already submitted yourself to Jesus? In what areas are you still holding on to control? Where might He be inviting you to deeper surrender?

Read: Matthew 16:21–28

Sit with this passage. What stands out to you?
Is there something God might be saying directly to your heart today?

Close your time in prayer.

Ask God to show you where you're still relying on self and striving for control. Invite Him to shape your heart into one of true surrender and obedience.

Action Step:

Write down one area of your life where you sense God is asking you to deny yourself and follow Him more fully. This might be something you need to give up, step into, or trust Him with. Pray over it and ask for the courage to take a practical step toward surrender this week.

Day 3: How's Your Prayer Life?

Jesus taught His disciples a framework for prayer—what we now call the Lord's Prayer. But before teaching how to pray, He first taught how not to pray. He warned against two common but misguided approaches: the prayers of the hypocrites, who prayed for show, and the babbling of the pagans, who believed that long, empty phrases would win them favor.

Read: Matthew 6:5–15

What's wrong with these two approaches to prayer?
What was Jesus correcting in the hearts of those who prayed this way?

Verse 8 says, *"Do not be like them, for your Father knows what you need before you ask him."*
How might your prayer life change if you approached God with deep trust that He already knows what you need—even before you ask?

Would your prayers be different if you believed that prayer is meant to draw you closer to God—not just tell Him what you want?
Think about the things you usually pray about. How would you summarize the themes or focus of your prayers?

Jesus drew a sharp contrast between those who use prayer to get things from God and those who use prayer to get *closer* to

God. The hypocrites and pagans were motivated by recognition or reward. But Jesus invites us to pray in a way that deepens our relationship with our Father.

Prayer isn't a transaction—it's a connection. It's not just a way to get what we want; it's the means by which we know God more.

When we adopt that mindset, the Lord's Prayer becomes a beautiful model of how to pray in a way that brings us near to God:

- We connect with God as our Loving Father – *"Our Father in heaven"*
- We adore Him and remember His holiness – *"Hallowed be your name"*
- We invite His will and His presence into our lives – *"Your kingdom come… on earth as it is in heaven"*
- We present our needs – *"Give us today our daily bread"*
- We confess our sins – *"Forgive us our debts, as we also have forgiven our debtors"*
- We ask for guidance and protection – *"Lead us not into temptation, but deliver us from the evil one"*

Which of these six elements tend to dominate your prayer life?
Are there any that are often missing from your prayers?

Prayer can be both beautifully simple and deeply challenging. It's simple because God is always inviting us to come to Him. Yet it's challenging because it requires trust, focus, vulnerability, and consistency. We must choose to show up and engage.

What part of prayer feels hardest for you? Is it doubt? Distraction? Insecurity? Busyness? God wants to hear about all of it—and He wants to meet you right where you are.

Close your time in prayer.

Speak honestly with God. Share what you struggle with in your prayer life, and ask Him to draw you closer. Invite Him to reshape your understanding of prayer as a way to be with Him, not just speak to Him.

Action Step:

Choose one element of the Lord's Prayer that is usually missing from your prayer life—adoration, confession, asking for guidance, etc.—and intentionally focus on that the next time you pray.

Day 4: You Are a Fisher of Men

Read: Luke 5:1–11

In verse 4, what was Jesus demonstrating about Himself to Peter?

How did Peter respond to Jesus—and why do you think he responded this way? What does his reaction reveal about his view of himself and of Jesus?

In verse 10, Jesus tells Peter that he will now *catch people*. What does that mean in the context of discipleship? What do you think Jesus is inviting Peter—and us—into?

Verse 11 tells us that the disciples left *everything* and followed Him. Notice that this moment of surrender comes right after an incredible catch—arguably one of their greatest professional successes as fishermen.

What did they give up? What might that have cost them?

Discipleship is not always easy. Following Jesus may come with a cost—comfort, control, reputation, or worldly success. But Jesus is clear and honest about the nature of the road we're called to walk.

Read: Mark 8:27–35

We are invited to follow Jesus on the road less traveled. What does that road look like in your life?

Read: Matthew 10:34–39

Conclude your time today by quietly reflecting on these words from Jesus.
What might He be saying to *you* through this passage?

Close your time in prayer.

Ask God to give you the courage to follow Jesus wholeheartedly—even when it costs you something. Ask for clarity, boldness, and a heart that is willing to leave anything behind for the sake of His calling.

Action Step:

Write down one thing in your life that might be holding you back from fully following Jesus—something you've been clinging to, avoiding, or afraid to surrender. Prayerfully ask the Lord to help you release it and take the next step forward as His disciple.

Day 5: Give Me a Mind Governed by the Spirit

We have all sinned and fall short of the glory of God. But where did that sin originate—and what can be done about it?

Read: Romans 3:22–24 and Romans 5:12

These verses help us understand the origin and universality of sin. Now consider the effects of sin on our mindset and spiritual direction:

Read: Romans 8:5–8

> *"Those who are dominated by the sinful nature think about sinful things, but those who are controlled by the Holy Spirit think about things that please the Spirit. So letting your sinful nature control your mind leads to death. But letting the Spirit control your mind leads to life and peace. For the sinful nature is always hostile to God. It never did obey God's laws, and it never will. That's why those who are still under the control of their sinful nature can never please God."*

There are times when we live "according to the flesh"—when our thoughts revolve around what we want right now, what we think will make us happy, admired, successful, or in control.

Can you recall specific times in your life when your thoughts and actions were led by the sinful nature rather than the

Spirit? What was the situation? How did you feel in the moment—and how did you feel afterward?

Now consider the opposite. Can you think of a time when you were living in step with the Spirit? When your decisions, words, or thoughts were aligned with God's will and reflected His character? Did you experience the peace that Romans 8 describes?

When we live with minds not governed by the Spirit, sin takes root. And while all of us sin, we often struggle to live in the reality of God's forgiveness. That's where the spiritual practice of confession becomes essential—not because God needs it, but because *we* need it to become who He's shaping us to be.

Read: 1 John 1:7–9

How does God respond to those who confess their sins to Him?

Many Christian thinkers have pointed to what's commonly referred to as the *Seven Deadly Sins*—a list of sins from which nearly all others tend to flow:

- Pride
- Envy
- Anger
- Sloth (laziness)
- Greed
- Gluttony
- Lust

These sins often begin in our thoughts and attitudes before they ever show up in our behavior.

Which of these do you struggle with most?
Can you trace sinful actions or unhealthy patterns in your life back to thoughts or attitudes that preceded them?

Spend time now in confession before God.
Use the following passages for reflection based on your personal areas of struggle:

- Pride: 1 Peter 5:4–5, James 4:4–6, Jeremiah 9:23–24
- Envy: Proverbs 14:30, James 3:14–16, 1 Corinthians 13:4
- Anger: Psalm 37:8, Ephesians 4:26, Proverbs 14:17
- Sloth: Proverbs 10:5, 2 Thessalonians 3:6–10, Proverbs 24:30–34
- Greed: Mark 10:17–25, Luke 12:15, Matthew 6:24
- Gluttony: Ezekiel 16:49, Proverbs 23:19–21, 1 Corinthians 6:19–20
- Lust: Matthew 5:28, 1 Corinthians 6:13, 2 Timothy 2:22

Close your time in prayer

Bring your specific struggles to God. Thank Him for His grace and forgiveness. Ask Him to renew your mind and give you a heart that desires what the Spirit desires.

Action Step:

Choose one of the seven deadly sins that you identified as an area of struggle. Write out a relevant verse from the list above and place it somewhere visible this week. Use it as a daily reminder to confess, pray, and invite the Spirit to govern your thoughts and choices.

Week 4

Training to be Like Christ

Day 1: You Are a Work in Progress

Read: Ephesians 2:1–10

"For we are God's masterpiece..." (some translations say "handiwork")

God has created each of us with intention, care, and purpose—we are His workmanship. But when we honestly reflect on our lives, we often feel like we're falling short. We wish we were better spouses, parents, children, friends, coworkers... better disciples of Christ.

Maybe you're not the parent you hoped to be.
Maybe you feel like you're not hitting your goals.
Maybe you're frustrated that you're not growing spiritually the way you long to.

Where do you feel most lacking or in need of growth right now?

The good news is: God isn't done with you. He wants to transform you, and He is faithful to complete the work He began. He desires to shape you into the best version of the person He created you to be. You are His masterpiece *in progress.*

What are your spiritual hopes for the future?

How do you hope to grow in your walk with God?

What does the best version of *you* look like?

Read: 1 John 2:6:

"Whoever claims to live in him must live as Jesus did."

To be truly transformed as Christians, we must learn to think like Jesus, perceive the world as He does, love what He loves, and obey as He obeyed. True transformation happens from the inside out—our faith begins in the heart and expresses itself through our daily actions.

If God were to completely transform your inner life, what would be different outwardly?

How would your actions, words, or habits shift to reflect that inner change?

Read: James 2:14–26

Conclude your time in Scripture by reflecting on this passage about living out our faith.

Close your time in prayer.

Thank God for calling you His masterpiece. Ask Him to continue His work in you, and surrender any discouragement about where you are today. Pray for strength and faith to grow in the direction He is leading.

Action Step:

Write down one character trait or spiritual habit that you want God to shape in you this week. Post it somewhere visible as a daily reminder that He is not finished with you—you are a work in progress, and He is still molding you.

Day 2: Fruit on the Vine

Read: Psalm 1

This psalm paints a picture of the blessed person—someone rooted, thriving, and spiritually fruitful.

According to verses 1–2, what does this person *avoid*?

In your own words, what does it mean to *delight in the law of the Lord*?

Read: Galatians 5:22–26

Now return to Psalm 1:3:

"That person is like a tree planted by streams of water,
which yields its fruit in season
and whose leaf does not wither—
whatever they do prospers."

What does this image teach us about how spiritual fruit is produced and nurtured in our lives?

"Whatever they do prospers."
What might this kind of fruitfulness and spiritual prosperity look like in your life?

Read: John 15:1–11

Jesus describes Himself as the *true vine*, and we are the branches.
What does it mean to *remain* in the vine?

What happens when we don't remain in Him?

What happens when we do?

Pruning is a necessary part of bearing more fruit.
Have you experienced God's pruning in your life before—seasons where something was removed, reshaped, or refined so you could grow spiritually?

Is there anything in your life right now that God may be trying to prune?

Where might He be inviting you to trust Him more deeply in the process?

Close your time in prayer.

Ask the Lord to help you remain in Him, to delight in His Word, and to welcome His pruning. Invite Him to reveal what needs to be uprooted or nourished so that your life can bear lasting fruit.

Action Step:

Choose one specific spiritual fruit from Galatians 5 (love, joy, peace, patience, kindness, goodness, faithfulness, gentleness, or self-control). Reflect on how this fruit could grow in your life this week—and write down one practical way to nurture it in your thoughts, words, or actions.

Day 3: Your Habits Shape Who You Become

Read: Galatians 5:22–23, 2 Corinthians 10:5, & Matthew 6:25–34

Just as daily health habits—what we eat, how we move, and how we rest—can shape us physically, our spiritual habits shape us spiritually.
We are always being changed, for better or for worse.
Change is a given; progress has to be worked for.

How might some of your daily practices be forming you spiritually—either drawing you closer to God or slowly pulling you away from Him?
How can spiritual disciplines such as Bible study, prayer, rest and Sabbath, and serving others transform your life over time?

Let's take a closer look at some of the core spiritual disciplines. For each one, reflect on both the impact it *can* have in your life, and the effect its *absence* may cause over time.

What effect would more time spent with this discipline have on your life?
What effect would the lack of this discipline have?

Discipline	More Time With It Would…	Without It I Might…
Bible Study		
Prayer		
Rest / Sabbath		
Serving Others		

Take a moment to reflect on your answers. These habits shape who you're becoming.

Galatians 5:22–23 reminds us that a life lived in step with the Spirit will bear fruit:

"But the fruit of the Spirit is love, joy, peace, patience, kindness, goodness, faithfulness, gentleness and self-control."

Which of these fruits do you feel God is calling you to strengthen right now?
Pick one to intentionally focus on over the next week or two.

Think of two or three specific situations in your daily life where you would like to see that fruit grow and blossom.

2 Corinthians 10:5 says:

"We take captive every thought to make it obedient to Christ."

This verse reminds us that spiritual growth also means training our minds. What we dwell on—about ourselves, others, or life—shapes our attitudes and actions.

What thoughts might you need to take captive right now to better reflect the mind of Christ and grow in the fruit of the Spirit?

Thoughts about myself:

Thoughts about others:

Thoughts about difficult or trying life circumstances:

Without intentional spiritual discipline, we risk drifting into complacency. Joy can fade. Patience can grow thin. Kindness can wear out.
That's why training matters.

How might focusing your time, energy, and thoughts on things like work, money, image, or busyness—rather than on God—distract you from growing spiritually?

Read: Matthew 6:25–34

Close your time in prayer.

The Lord to help you develop habits that draw you closer to Him—habits that renew your mind, strengthen your character, and produce spiritual fruit. Invite Him to reveal areas of your life where small, daily changes could lead to long-term transformation. Ask for His help in taking every thought captive and remaining rooted in His truth.

Action Step:

Choose one specific spiritual discipline—Bible study, prayer, Sabbath rest, or serving others.
Write down one intentional way you can incorporate this habit into your routine this week.
Then choose one fruit of the Spirit (love, joy, peace, patience, kindness, goodness, faithfulness, gentleness, or self-control) to intentionally cultivate in your thoughts, words, or actions.

Day 4: God, Help Me Grow

Read: 2 Timothy 3

In this chapter, Paul warns Timothy that "in the last days difficult times will come." He goes on to describe a long list of characteristics we often associate with people who are clearly living far from God—selfish, arrogant, abusive, greedy, slanderous, lacking self-control. But the most sobering part of the passage is verse 5: "having a form of godliness but denying its power." These aren't necessarily enemies of the Church. They might be the very ones sitting beside us in church. They might appear spiritual or even be involved in ministry, yet they lack the true power of a transformed life.

It's easy to read this list and think, "I know someone like that!" or "That sounds like the culture around me." But Paul isn't just pointing fingers—he's prompting self-examination. Do we ever settle for the appearance of godliness without yielding to the power of God? Do we sometimes cling to our own version of religion while resisting the life-changing work of the Holy Spirit?

The truth is, we all need that deep transformation only God can bring. His power doesn't just clean us up on the outside—it reshapes our hearts, our desires, our thoughts, and our actions.

As you read verses 1–4 again, ask the Holy Spirit to gently show you any ways these traits might still be present in your own life. Ask Him to replace pride with humility, selfishness with service, and emptiness with real relationship.

Later in the chapter, Paul reminds Timothy of the power and purpose of God's Word: "All Scripture is God-breathed and is useful for teaching, rebuking, correcting and training in righteousness." (v. 16) God's Word is not a checklist or an old book of rules. It is living, powerful, and intended to shape us into people who are equipped for every good work.

Reread verses 16–17. Paul reminds us that *"All Scripture is God-breathed."* That means the Word of God isn't just helpful—it's holy, alive, and powerful. It shapes us when we allow it to teach, convict, and correct us.

How is Scripture useful to you in these ways?

Teaching ________________________________

Rebuking ________________________________

Correcting ______________________________

Training ________________________________

And how does Scripture equip you for every good work?

We are God's servants, equipped by His Word to carry out the good works He's prepared for us. To do so, we must remain faithful, stay grounded in truth, and continue running the race with endurance.

Read: Hebrews 12:1–3

We are not running this race alone. Christ has gone before us, and His Spirit empowers us to keep moving forward. Even in a culture that drifts further from God, we are being equipped to persevere in faith, live with integrity, and boldly reflect the heart of Christ.

Close your time in prayer.

Thank the Lord for His powerful Word and for the way it transforms hearts and lives. Ask Him to remove anything false or shallow in your faith and to replace it with a vibrant, growing relationship. Invite Him to equip you with perseverance and purpose as you follow Him more fully.

Action Step:

Choose one of the characteristics listed in verses 1–4 that stood out to you today. Ask God to help you uproot it from your heart—and then write down one practical action you can take this week to pursue the opposite fruit of the Spirit in your thoughts, words, or habits.

Day 5: Learning to Love Like Jesus

Read: Romans 6:3–14

God's desire isn't simply for outward behavior change—it's for a complete remaking of who we are. He wants us to live and love as Jesus would if He were walking in our shoes. According to this passage in Romans, how is that possible?

How does this passage tell you it's possible to live and love like Jesus?

Read: Ephesians 2:10

What truth stands out to you from this verse?

Now consider this: Jesus never taught that transformation happens through religious performance. Instead, He focused on the heart—and on actions rooted in compassion.

Read: Luke 10:25–37

How would you summarize the message of this parable in your own words?

Who is your neighbor? Be honest. Who do you sometimes view as a "Samaritan"—someone who is difficult for you to love or understand? Why is it challenging? And how might you show them love and mercy?

Jesus didn't just say He loved people—He showed it. He healed, served, taught, forgave, wept, washed feet, and died for sinners. His love was visible, sacrificial, and powerful.

"A new command I give you: Love one another. As I have loved you, so you must love one another.
By this everyone will know that you are my disciples, if you love one another." John 13:34–35

Jesus sets the standard: *Love as I have loved you.* It's a calling we can't fulfill on our own. But we're not meant to—we are empowered by the Holy Spirit to love like Jesus.

Still, it isn't always easy. Some people are simply hard to love. You may have individuals in your life that bring up frustration, hurt, or anger. It could be a relative, a coworker, a former friend, or someone from your past.

Take a moment to reflect. Who comes to mind? What situations trigger those reactions in you? Write down the names or scenarios you sense God is bringing to your attention.

Bring these to the Lord in prayer. Lay them at His feet. And listen for the Spirit whispering:
"You don't need to manufacture this love. Let Me love them through you."

Close your time in prayer.

Ask the Lord to show you how to love like Him—not in your own strength, but through the power of the Holy Spirit. Invite Him to reveal any hardness in your heart and ask for the grace to extend love, even when it's difficult.

Action Step:

Choose one person or situation from your list above. Each day this week, pray specifically for them and ask God to give you one opportunity to show love in a tangible way. Whether it's through a kind word, a prayer, a gesture, or a new attitude—take a small step forward in loving like Jesus.

Week 5

Humility, Servanthood, & Community

Day 1: Humility is a Gift

"Humility, if we could ever grow into it, would not be a burden. It would be an immense gift. Humility is the freedom to stop trying to be what we're not, or pretending to be what we're not, and accepting our 'appropriate smallness.' In Luther's words, humility is the decision to 'let God be God.'"
—John Ortberg

Read: Philippians 2:1–11

This passage paints a powerful picture of Christlike humility. Jesus, though fully God, emptied Himself, took on the nature of a servant, and became obedient even to death on a cross.

Why is humility so vital to having a heart that is open to being used by God?

Pride is the opposite of humility. It resists surrender, clings to control, and subtly elevates self above others.

Pride often shows up in subtle ways in our daily lives. Take a moment to reflect: which of these expressions of pride do you recognize in yourself?

- Becoming preoccupied with appearance or reputation
- Being overly concerned with what others think
- Insisting on being right
- Valuing your opinion above others'
- Rejecting correction or becoming defensive
- Looking down on or excluding others
- Putting your own needs first

Which of these prideful tendencies do you notice most in yourself? When or with whom are you most likely to struggle in this area?

Read: John 13:1–17

In this passage, Jesus kneels to wash His disciples' feet. The King of kings takes the posture of a servant. He models the very humility that He calls us to live out.

When you hear the word "servanthood," what comes to mind?
Is this a role you gladly embrace, or does it go against your natural instincts?

We may never be called to humble ourselves to the degree that Jesus did, but we're presented with mini-opportunities for servanthood every single day.

We humble ourselves when we:

- Welcome an interruption to our schedule
- Hold our tongue in frustration
- Help someone without expecting anything in return
- Show patience, especially when it's hard
- Love someone who's difficult to love

What are some other small, everyday ways you can demonstrate humility and servanthood?

Close your time in prayer.

God to reveal any hidden pride in your life. Ask Him to give you the mind of Christ and to help you see others through His eyes. Ask Him to help you choose humility and servanthood, even when it costs you comfort, control, or convenience. Invite the Holy Spirit to transform your heart and guide you throughout the week ahead.

Action Step:

Look for one mini-opportunity today to humble yourself and serve someone else. Don't wait for it to be convenient. Choose to follow Jesus' example in a real, tangible way.

Jot down any thoughts or prayers that come to mind as you spend time with Him.

Day 2: Spiritual Transformation

Read: Acts 9:1–19

Paul moved from completely opposing the cause of Christ—persecuting and even killing Jesus' disciples—to becoming one of the most important leaders in the first generation of Christians. His entire life trajectory changed when he encountered Jesus on the road to Damascus. While Paul made a conscious decision to repent, this transformation didn't occur by his own strength alone. Paul was spiritually transformed during his encounter with Christ—he became someone entirely new.

We often refer to this kind of change as *spiritual transformation.* It is the process of becoming who God intended us to be, made possible through Christ.

Read: 2 Corinthians 5:17

What are some "old things" that have passed away in your life?

What "new things" have you experienced since encountering Jesus?

The transformation we experience when we first accept Jesus is called *justification.* This legal term reflects the truth that we are guilty because of our sin, yet fully forgiven through Christ. We are made right in God's eyes—not because of anything we've done, but because we are covered in the righteousness of Jesus.

Read the following verses. How do they help deepen your understanding of justification?

Romans 5:9–10

"Since we have now been justified by his blood, how much more shall we be saved from God's wrath through him! For if, while we were God's enemies, we were reconciled to him through the death of his Son, how much more, having been reconciled, shall we be saved through his life!"

Hebrews 9:19–22

"When Moses had proclaimed every command of the law to all the people, he took the blood of calves, together with water, scarlet wool and branches of hyssop, and sprinkled the scroll and all the people… In fact, the law requires that nearly everything be cleansed with blood, and without the shedding of blood there is no forgiveness."

Romans 5:6–9

"You see, at just the right time, when we were still powerless, Christ died for the ungodly… God demonstrates his own love for us in this: While we were still sinners, Christ died for us. Since we have now been justified by his blood, how much more shall we be saved from God's wrath through him!"

Galatians 2:15–16

"We… know that a person is not justified by the works of the law, but by faith in Jesus Christ. So we, too, have put our faith in Christ Jesus that we may be justified by faith in Christ and not by the works of the law, because by the works of the law no one will be justified."

Justification is just the beginning. After we place our faith in Jesus, we begin the lifelong process of *sanctification*—being continually shaped and transformed into the image of Christ.

2 Corinthians 3:18

And we all, who with unveiled faces contemplate the Lord's glory, are being transformed into his image with ever-increasing glory, which comes from the Lord, who is the Spirit."

Do you feel like you've regularly experienced transformation since following Jesus? Why or why not?

What obstacles are currently in the way of you having a deeper spiritual transformation?

Close your time in prayer.

Ask the Lord to continue shaping your heart, opening your eyes to areas of growth, and removing any obstacles that keep you from experiencing full transformation.

Action step:

Reflect on one area of your life where you know God is calling you to change. Write it down, and ask Him to begin transforming that area starting today.

Day 3: The Heart of a Servant

In place of pride, Jesus invites us to live a life of humility. Humility isn't about convincing ourselves or others that we're less. It's not about trying to make ourselves feel insignificant or unimportant. Humility is the freedom to stop pretending to be what we're not. It's the freedom to embrace the person God created us to be. Humility isn't thinking less of yourself—it's thinking of yourself less.

We can consider pride the opposite of humility. Pride often shows up in subtle ways that hinder our ability to live and love like Jesus. Would you benefit from finding freedom from any of the following?

- Always being concerned about what others think of you
- Feeling criticized when others correct you or call you out on a mistake or shortcoming
- Struggling with feelings of criticism or judgment toward others
- Trying to be better than others, trying to be special, trying to be something you're not

Read: Mark 9:33–37

How does the world define greatness? Usually by power, prestige, possessions, and position. But Jesus measures greatness entirely differently. He teaches that true greatness is found through service—not status.

In this passage, Jesus is essentially saying: "Here's your ministry. Here's how you make your life great. Give yourself to those who can give you no status and no prestige. Give yourself to others in service—not to receive power or position, but out of love. Welcome this child, help this child, serve this child—not just for the child's sake, but for your sake. Otherwise, your life will be wasted on a quest for greatness as the world defines it. When you love and serve simply for the joy of it, it's then that you will begin to understand how life in the kingdom works."

If the child in this passage represents someone who brings you no reward or status, who might that be in your life? Who could you be called to help or serve—even in small, seemingly insignificant ways—that won't give you anything in return?

Pride can rob us of our ability to love others sincerely. It often leads us to exclude others instead of embracing them. Think specifically:

- Who are the people you tend to keep at arm's distance?
- Who are you tempted to see yourself as superior to?
- How is pride at the center of that behavior?
- Are the people from the question above the same as those you listed in the prior question?

Jesus measured greatness in terms of service, not status. Are you living as a servant? Reflect on the questions below:

- Do you make yourself available to serve?
- Are you willing to help even when it's inconvenient?
- Do you become resentful when your schedule is interrupted?

- Do you do the best with what you have?
- Do you make the most of your time and resources? Or do you tend to procrastinate, make excuses, or wait for the "right time" to serve?
- Do you recognize the importance of serving in small ways?

Jesus didn't consider any task beneath Him—He washed feet, served lepers, cooked breakfast. He came to serve.

- Do you have a heart that's willing to serve in quiet, simple, unnoticed ways?
- Do you serve without needing the approval or applause of others?
- Do you serve for an audience of One, or do you desire recognition and esteem?

Close your time in prayer.

Ask God to show you how He's calling you to live more humbly, and to serve more freely. Invite Him to reveal areas where pride is getting in the way of deeper connection with Him and with others.

Action step:

Choose one small, humble act of service you can do for someone today—especially someone who won't give you anything in return. Do it quietly and joyfully, knowing this is the kind of greatness Jesus celebrates.

Day 4: Live What You Believe

Read: Matthew 5:1–2 and Matthew 7:24–29

In these two passages, Jesus calls His followers to more than just belief—He calls them to obedience. It's not enough to simply hear His words. True discipleship is proven through action. We are called to build our lives on the solid foundation of His truth by putting it into practice.

Throughout His teachings, Jesus often challenged cultural norms and religious expectations. He would begin with the phrase, "You have heard that it was said," referencing long-standing traditions or laws, then follow it with, "But I tell you," pointing His followers to a new way of living—one shaped by the heart of God, not the approval of the world.

As His disciples, we are called to shape the world around us, not conform to it.

Read: Matthew 5:1–12

Which of Jesus' statements in the Beatitudes do you find most countercultural? Why?

Is there a particular category of "blessed" with which you most identify?

What are you most challenged by in this teaching?

Jesus doesn't invite us to be mere students—interested observers of His wisdom. He calls us to be disciples. A student may seek knowledge for knowledge's sake, but a disciple learns in order to obey. This is why Jesus frequently warned His followers to examine the fruit their lives were producing.

He didn't just want listeners. He wanted people whose lives reflected the transformation that comes from knowing Him.

Read: Matthew 7:15–17

When have you experienced the tension between believing something to be true and living it out?

What does this passage say about what others should see in your life if you're truly following Jesus?

Close your time in prayer.

Ask God to reveal any areas where you've been content to simply hear His words without acting on them. Invite Him to help you live with bold obedience and produce fruit that reflects your faith.

Action step:

Choose one teaching of Jesus from the Beatitudes or the Sermon on the Mount and intentionally put it into practice today. Let it shape your choices, your attitude, and your interactions with others.

Day 5: Well Done, Good and Faithful Servant

Read: Matthew 6:1–4

One of the great spiritual practices in serving and loving others is learning to do so quietly and humbly—without seeking recognition. When we allow ourselves to serve others in love without the need to be noticed, we gain freedom from the pressure to impress. We begin to let go of the craving for praise and approval, and instead root our identity in God alone.

Think about some of your current opportunities to be used by God in quiet, unseen ways. How might you love and serve others without expecting a thank you or applause? This doesn't mean you can't appreciate a kind word of thanks—it simply means that the thank you isn't your reason for doing it.

Here are a few ways to practice serving in secret:

- Pick up after someone around the house without grumbling
- Make a cup of tea or coffee for someone without being asked
- Send a note of encouragement to someone who may need it
- Pray for someone consistently without telling them about it
- Make a quiet donation to someone in need

- Do a task for someone at home, work, or in your neighborhood with no expectation of acknowledgment

Write a few examples of how you could intentionally serve and love others quietly this week:

Read: Matthew 25:31–46

Jesus' words here can be challenging. He makes it clear that our faith is lived out in the way we love and serve those in need. This kind of service isn't glamorous. Often, it's inconvenient. Sometimes, it's uncomfortable. And yet, it is where true discipleship is revealed.

How does this passage challenge you? When is the last time you served someone our culture might consider "the least"?

Would the way you serve others look different if you truly believed that, in doing so, you were serving Jesus Himself? How?

Now pause and reflect—how well do you receive acts of service from others? Is it easy or difficult for you?

How might receiving acts of service actually help you grow in humility?

Can you grow in humility by freely serving others without expecting anything in return—and also by receiving help with grace and gratitude? How so?

Read: Matthew 25:21

Close your time in prayer. Ask God to help you grow in humility, to release your desire for attention and approval, and to cultivate a heart that serves for His glory alone. May your aim be to hear the words, "Well done, good and faithful servant," as you grow in loving others without the need to be seen.

Action step:

Choose one intentional act of service today that you can do quietly. Don't announce it. Don't seek credit. Do it purely as an act of love and worship.

Week 6

Living for Christ

Day 1: Is Comfort Your Primary Objective?

Read: James 1:2–4, Proverbs 4:23

Do you often feel your schedule is out of control? What feels out of balance for you?

What would a more balanced life look like if you were to have one?

Do you think God wants you to have a more balanced life? Why or why not?

Consider this for a moment: We are told in our culture that we are to seek a balanced life. This means that we seek a life that is pleasant and comfortable. We have church on Sundays, work during the week, relaxation on the weekends. A time blocked off for exercise, a checkmark for a completed Bible study, and portions of ourselves, our energy, and our personality are allocated for each of the different roles we play in our day. There's church-me, work-me, mom-me, happy-hour-me. We seek lives that are manageable, secure, and overall pleasant.

But perhaps that's not God's ultimate goal for our lives. God is far less concerned with our comfort than He is with our growth. Really consider that for a moment.

Think about some struggles you've had—times you've been upset, angry, frustrated, or disappointed. In those situations, were you seeking comfort and balance? Was your primary goal to get or return to a place of happiness and security?

And in those very situations, might God's primary goal have been to develop your perseverance, character, and faith rather than simply return you to a place of security and happiness?

God allows challenges and hardships in our lives because He seeks to cultivate something far more important than balance—He seeks to cultivate a heart that desires above all else to live for Him. Colossians 3:17 tells us that whatever we do, whether in word or deed, we are to do it ALL in the name of the Lord.

Trials and difficulties in our lives develop perseverance, which in turn produces character and makes our faith mature and complete.

What are your most recent—or current—trials that God may be using to make your faith mature and complete?

When we go through trials and difficult times, we always have the option to become bitter, angry, discouraged, and/or defeated. We need to constantly be aware of the choice we have in our responses to our troubles and hardships.

"Above all else, guard your heart,
for everything you do flows from it."
Proverbs 4:23

What does it mean to you to "guard your heart"?

Considering your response from the previous question about recent trials, what has your response to those trials been?
In what ways could you guard your heart during difficult times?
Are there actions that you could take that would help to guard your heart?

In what areas of your life does your heart feel unguarded, unprotected, or not connected with God?

Close your time in prayer.

Ask God to show you where your desire for comfort has outweighed your desire for growth. Ask Him to strengthen your faith, deepen your perseverance, and help you guard your heart as you live fully for Him.

Action step:

Identify one area of your life this week where you tend to prioritize comfort. Take one intentional step in that area to choose obedience, sacrifice, or growth instead—and invite God to meet you there.

Day 2: Disciples Follow Jesus

Have you ever had a conversation with someone who was constantly checking their phone, unable to give you their full attention? It can be a frustrating feeling to try to talk to and connect with someone, but to know their attention is only partially on you and what you're saying. Having half of someone's attention can feel like you have none of it at all.

Do you think God ever feels that way about you? Is it possible that He wants to connect with you, listen to you and guide you, but you're consumed with your job, distracted by stress, focused on pursuing pleasure or mindless relaxation, or maybe just on your phone?

True disciples prioritize pursuing and following God. It's not enough to simply want His truth; we must go after it.

How do you put yourself in a position to hear from and connect with God? What habits or activities do you partake in that put you in a position to give Him attention and be open to His voice and teaching?

And what habits or activities prevent you from positioning yourself to hear from God? In other words, when are you least likely to be able to hear what He has to say?

Read: Matthew 17:1–13

Notice that in order to more deeply experience Jesus, the disciples had to make an effort. They spent time and energy to follow Jesus up the mountain in order to be in the right place to learn from Him, and the reward was incredible.

What did the disciples learn from Jesus in these verses?

Disciples of Jesus don't just listen to Him; they do what He says.

Read: Matthew 7:21:

"Not everyone who says to Me, 'Lord, Lord!' will enter the kingdom of heaven, but only the one who does the will of My Father in heaven."

What does Jesus mean when He says the one who does "the will of My Father in heaven"?

Obeying God must go beyond simply doing the right things. God has never been impressed with people who do the right things for the wrong reasons.

Read: Isaiah 1:11 & 15

When you read these verses from Matthew 7 and Isaiah 1, what emotions do you experience? Do any questions come to mind?

Jesus taught that it is our *fruit* that separates true disciples from those who are simply going through the motions.

How does what He taught expand upon a similar idea found in Isaiah 1?

Read: Isaiah 1:16–20

What kind of "fruit" are mentioned in these verses from those who follow God?

Following and obeying Jesus requires more than brief spurts of righteousness. We don't produce fruit simply by trying harder—remaining peaceful for a few minutes so we can prove we love God. The fruit of the Spirit is naturally cultivated in our lives when we genuinely follow Jesus, submit ourselves to His teaching, and allow ourselves to be led by Him throughout the course of our days.

Following Jesus doesn't simply mean doing more good things. It means abiding so closely in Him that our good deeds are simply evidence that God is working in our lives and in our hearts.

Read: Galatians 5:22–23:

"But the fruit of the Spirit is love, joy, peace, patience, kindness, goodness, faithfulness, gentleness and self-control. Against such things there is no law."

Which fruit of the Spirit are most evident in your life?

Which fruit of the Spirit are least evident in your life? Where is God calling you to grow?

Close your time in prayer.

Ask God to help you be fully present with Him. Invite Him to cultivate the fruit of the Spirit in your life by drawing you nearer to Him. Confess any areas of divided attention and ask for renewed focus on His will.

Action step:

Choose one distraction to remove this week—something that's been pulling your focus from the life God is calling you to live. Whether it's mindless scrolling, background noise, or overscheduling, choose one way to clear space for deeper connection and obedience.

Day 3: Are You Living in the Name of Jesus?

Read: Matthew 6:19–24

If your goal is to seek a *balanced heart*—not just a balanced life—then you must learn to love:

- the right things
- to the right degree
- in the right way
- with the right kind of love

Reflect:

Wealth, work, beauty, talents, and pleasure are all blessings from God. But do you love or pursue any of them in the wrong way or to the wrong extent?

On the flip side, are there people or things you aren't loving *to the right degree*, *in the right way*, or *with the right kind of love*?

In what areas of your life does your heart feel unbalanced?

Achieving a balanced heart requires intentional effort. Like running a race, it takes purpose, focus, and perseverance.

Consider the following questions:

- When and where will I pray? What will my quiet time with God look like?
- How can I approach work in a way that reflects Christ?

- How can I use my money to honor God?
- How can I spend my time in a way that honors God?
- How can I engage in Christian community for fellowship and accountability?
- With whom can I grow in love and patience, truly loving as Jesus would?

Which of these questions speaks to you most right now? How do you want to respond?

Read: Colossians 3:17:

"Whatever you do, in word or deed, do everything in the name of the Lord Jesus, giving thanks to God the Father through Him."

What does it mean to do something *in the name of Jesus*?

In biblical terms, a person's name reflects their character. To do something in the name of Jesus means doing it in His character—loving like Him, responding like Him, speaking and thinking like Him.

Reflect on the everyday:

- What would it mean to wake up each morning in Jesus' name?
- What would your first thoughts be?
- What would it look like to do your job (or care for your home, study, etc.) in Jesus' name?
- What would it look like to love your family in Jesus' name?
- What would it look like to drive in traffic, do chores, or browse social media in Jesus' name?
- How would Jesus respond to rude drivers, endless laundry, or unedifying entertainment?

Paul is clear—whatever you do, whether in word or deed, *do it in the name of Jesus*. Nothing is excluded.

Read: Matthew 6:33 & Matthew 10:37–39

Jesus never told His followers to seek a comfortable or balanced life. Instead, He called them to devotion, surrender, and daily obedience.

What does He say is worthy of your ultimate devotion?

Close your time in prayer

Talk with God about the areas of your life that feel unbalanced or misaligned with His character.
Ask Him to help you see how you can reflect Jesus more fully in your words, actions, and everyday moments.
Pray for strength to let go of any comforts or attachments that are taking precedence over your calling.

Action Step:

Choose one specific area of your life—work, family, routine, or time online—and commit to intentionally living it in the name of Jesus this week.

Day 4: Forming New Habits

Paul describes many processes involved in our spiritual transformation:

"For those God foreknew he also predestined to be conformed to the image of his Son, that he might be the firstborn among many brothers and sisters."
—Romans 8:29

"Do not conform to the pattern of this world, but be transformed by the renewing of your mind. Then you will be able to test and approve what God's will is—his good, pleasing and perfect will."
—Romans 12:2

"But the fruit of the Spirit is love, joy, peace, forbearance, kindness, goodness, faithfulness, gentleness and self-control. Against such things there is no law. Those who belong to Christ Jesus have crucified the flesh with its passions and desires. Since we live by the Spirit, let us keep in step with the Spirit."
—Galatians 5:22-25

Each of these verses highlights a different dimension of the process of spiritual growth: being conformed to the image of Christ, being transformed by the renewal of our minds, and being led by the Spirit to produce fruit—not by striving harder, but by surrendering more deeply.

Read: Ephesians 4:17–32

In Romans 12:2, Paul speaks of the "renewing of your mind." In Ephesians 4:23, he mentions the "attitude of your minds." What do you think the difference is between these two phrases? What is Paul calling us to reflect on?

Paul's instructions in Ephesians are not one-time changes but lifelong habits. The Christian life is a continual process of "putting off" the old self and "putting on" the new self. These instructions call us to actively remove behaviors and mindsets that no longer fit our identity in Christ—and to replace them with new actions that reflect His character.

One helpful way to view our sins is not simply as isolated actions but as repeated habits we've developed—patterns that don't reflect the holiness God calls us to.

Which phrases from Ephesians 4:17–32 describe sin as habitual?

Interestingly, the word *habit* comes from the Latin *habitus*, which referred to the clothing worn by a religious order. That clothing visually represented a commitment to a certain way of life. In the same way, Paul invites us to "put on" new habits—habits that show our commitment to holiness and to following Christ.

Look again at the list of habits you identified above. Which of your current habits might need to be replaced by ones that reflect your desire to grow in Christ?

Habits of the Old Nature:	
Habits I Should "Put On" Instead:	

Spiritual transformation doesn't happen overnight. There is no such thing as instant godliness. But over time, as we put off our old habits and put on new ones, we are shaped more and more into the likeness of Christ.

Close your time today in prayer. Ask God to reveal which habits are keeping you from growing. Ask Him for the strength, patience, and perseverance to form new ones that reflect your identity as His child.

Action step:

Choose one specific habit this week that reflects your old self and begin replacing it with a new one that reflects your commitment to walking in the way of Christ.

Day 5: Share the Good News

Think of a time when you received truly good news. How did it feel? What was your immediate response?

Now, read the following verses. What message do they have in common?

"And how can anyone preach unless they are sent? As it is written: 'How beautiful are the feet of those who bring good news!'"
—Romans 10:15

"But he said, 'I must proclaim the good news of the kingdom of God to the other towns also, because that is why I was sent.'"
—Luke 4:43

"The Spirit of the Sovereign Lord is on me, because the Lord has anointed me to proclaim good news to the poor. He has sent me to bind up the brokenhearted, to proclaim freedom for the captives and release from darkness for the prisoners..."
—Isaiah 61:1–2

"The blind receive sight, the lame walk, those who have leprosy are cleansed, the deaf hear, the dead are raised, and the good news is proclaimed to the poor."
—Matthew 11:5

Each of these verses points to the life-changing truth of the *gospel*—the good news that God has made a way for us to be forgiven, redeemed, and restored through Jesus.

How would you define the word "gospel" in one sentence?

Read: Acts 17:22–31

As you read Paul's message in Athens, what stands out to you? Is there anything that feels surprising, significant, or in need of deeper reflection?

Paul was speaking to a city full of idols, philosophies, and temples. Instead of condemning the culture, he started by engaging with it—looking for connection points to share the truth of Christ. Paul knew the gospel was not bound by geography or tradition. It is deeply personal, universally relevant, and always timely. His approach reminds us that the good news must be shared in a way people can understand.

Why is it important to understand the culture, values, and experiences of those with whom we share the gospel?

Read 1 Peter 3:15:

"Always be prepared to give an answer to everyone who asks you to give the reason for the hope that you have."

Spend a few quiet moments in prayer. Ask God to place someone specific on your heart—someone who needs to hear about the hope you've found in Christ.

Ask Him for boldness. For wisdom. For the words to speak.

Then—commit to being ready. The world needs more good news. Let your life, your actions, and your words be part of sharing it.

Keep pressing on toward the goal. Your transformation doesn't end here. As you reflect on the days you've spent in this study, remember: spiritual growth is not about perfection but about *direction*. You've shown up. You've opened your heart to God's Word. That is no small thing.

You've taken steps to become more grounded, more aware, more Christlike—not by your strength alone, but by walking in step with the Spirit. Keep building the habits. Keep renewing your mind. Keep seeking the One who transforms.

Now go—live it out, and share the good news.

Bonus

Spiritual Disciplines Leader Guide

Introduction

Leader Guide Contents

- Welcome
- Using the Leader Guide
- Weeks 1–6: Spiritual Disciplines
- About the Author

WELCOME

This Leader Guide is designed to help you facilitate meaningful, Christ-centered conversations as your group moves through the *Spiritual Disciplines* devotional series. Over these six weeks, you will explore practices that draw believers closer to God—such as meditating on Scripture, slowing down, prayer, confession, humility, servanthood, and living each day in the name of Jesus.

The goal of this study is not perfection, pressure, or performance. It's about helping each person learn to walk more closely with the Lord through the small, intentional habits that shape a life of spiritual growth.

As you lead, you'll be creating space for your group to reflect, share openly, pray together, and encourage one another in their daily pursuit of Christ.

"*Train yourself for godliness.*" — 1 Timothy 4:7
This study invites each of us to practice the rhythms that

make our hearts more attentive to God—one day, one step, one discipline at a time.

Leading Your Spiritual Disciplines Small Group

As you guide your group, your role is not to have all the answers but to create a welcoming and supportive environment where each person feels safe to share, reflect, and grow. The *Spiritual Disciplines* devotionals focus on daily practices that help believers experience God's presence more consistently and follow Him more closely.

This Leader Guide gives you the structure, support, and discussion prompts you need to help group members:

- reflect on what God is teaching them
- apply the themes to real-life situations
- take small, meaningful steps toward spiritual growth
- build community through honest conversation and encouragement.

Using This Guide

Each weekly session includes:

- **Scripture Reading & Discussion**
  Guided questions based on the devotionals help your group reflect on how the week's theme applies to everyday life.
- **Personal Application**
  Encourage members to consider practical ways they can live out the week's spiritual discipline—through small choices, habits, and intentional steps.
- **Accountability Check-In (optional)**
  If your group chooses to pair the devotionals with the SoulStrength Fit program, each week includes an

accountability check-in for workouts, nutrition, and daily habits. This allows the group to grow spiritually and physically while aligning all areas of life with God's design.

Closing Prayer

Each session ends with a simple prayer to bring the group's reflections and needs before the Lord.

Options for Group Study

Option 1: Using the Devotionals Alone

This guide offers everything you need to lead a meaningful small group focused entirely on the six weeks of *Spiritual Disciplines* devotionals. Each session encourages reflection, conversation, and spiritual formation.

Option 2: Pairing with SoulStrength Fit's Faith-Based Fitness Program

For a fully integrated experience, consider pairing the devotionals with the SoulStrength Fit faith-based strength-training program.

Each week's at-home workouts correspond with the devotionals, offering a practical way to connect worship, discipleship, and exercise in everyday life. This option helps participants grow in both body and spirit, forming habits that honor God physically, mentally, and spiritually.

Learn more at www.soulstrengthfit.com.

Tips for Leading Your Group

- **Create a welcoming atmosphere:** Encourage open sharing, listening, and mutual support.
- **Adapt as needed:** Adjust questions, pacing, or depth based on your group's needs.
- **Encourage reflection:** Allow silence and space for people to process.
- **Stay flexible:** Some discussions may go deeper than expected—let the Spirit lead.

- **Prioritize encouragement:** Remind each participant of God's love, patience, and ongoing work in their lives.

As a leader, your greatest role is to create space for God to work. Trust that He will guide your group's conversations, shape each heart, and draw every person closer to Him in each meeting.

Week 1

Meditating on Scripture

Spiritual Disciplines | Leader Guide – Week 1

Meditating on Scripture

Opening Prayer

Lord, thank You for bringing us together. We're here because we want to understand You better and learn what You're saying to us through Your Word. Help us slow down, quiet our minds, and be present with You. If there are places where we feel distracted, discouraged, or unsure where to start with Scripture, meet us there. Open our hearts to whatever You want to show us, and guide this conversation in a way that draws us closer to You. Amen.

Discussion Questions

Read: James 1:4–8

Currently, how do you feel about the time you dedicate to reading and meditating on Scripture?

- Are there any changes you'd like to make in this area? What might those look like?

Read: Romans 7:18–20

- Can you relate to the struggle Paul describes—wanting to do good, but struggling to carry it out?
- In what situations is this struggle the greatest for you?

- In what ways are you currently living out your walk as a disciple of Jesus?
- In what ways would you like to grow as one of Christ's disciples?

To be a disciple of Christ, we must first understand who He is and why He came. But true discipleship goes beyond comprehension—it requires participation. To follow Jesus is to join in His mission here on earth.

- John the Baptist took action by publicly proclaiming Jesus' identity.
- Andrew responded by immediately telling his brother, Simon, about the Messiah he had found.
- What has been your experience with talking to others about Jesus?
- What is one way you can participate in Jesus' mission this week—whether it's through a conversation, an act of service, or intentional prayer for someone who needs Christ?

Read: Luke 24:28–32

"Then their eyes were opened and they recognized him."

Sometimes we need help understanding Scripture. Sometimes we need help with our faith. Sometimes we need help seeing Jesus at work in our lives.

- Where do you need your eyes to be opened?
- How might you pray for the Holy Spirit to increase your understanding and strengthen your faith?

Accountability Check-In

(If pairing with the SoulStrength Fit workout program)

Workouts:

- Were you able to complete your workouts this week?
- What helped you stay on track—or what made it challenging?
- How did you feel physically, mentally, or spiritually after completing your workouts?

Nutrition:

- How did you feel about your nutrition choices this week?
- What went well, and what do you feel good about?
- Were there any moments where it was tough to stay on track?
- What got in the way?

Daily Habits:

- Let's reflect on other daily habits—like hydration, protein intake, or sleep. Which of these went well for you this week?
- Were there any areas that felt especially challenging (e.g., drinking enough water, getting enough sleep, or planning meals ahead)?
- Did you notice yourself turning to food, snacks, or drinks for comfort or stress relief?
- What might help you respond differently next time?

Looking Ahead:

- What is one goal you want to focus on this coming week—whether it's a workout, a mindset shift, or a small habit to improve your health and alignment with God's design?

- How can the group support you and help you stay accountable?

Closing Prayer

Invite group members to share one thing they'd like prayer for—something personal, practical, or spiritual. Close in prayer:

Lord, thank You for our time together. Help us stay close to You this week and understand Your Word in a deeper, clearer way. Be with each of us in the things we shared, and keep guiding our steps. Amen.

Week 2

Practice Slowing Down & Celebrating

Spiritual Disciplines | Leader Guide – Week 2

Practice Slowing Down & Celebrating

Opening Prayer

Lord, thank You for giving us this space to pause and be with You. We're often pulled in so many directions, and it's easy to move through life hurried and distracted. Help us slow down right now—quiet our thoughts, settle our hearts, and make room for Your peace. As we talk and reflect today, show us what it looks like to walk with You at Your pace. Amen.

Discussion Questions

Let's begin with a reflection on hurry and peace.
It's critical to realize that we cannot follow Jesus in a hurry. We can't think as He thinks, love as He loves, or act as He would act when we're constantly rushing. Hurry distracts us from God's presence and keeps us focused on tasks, problems, and pressure instead of truth, joy, and peace.

• When are you most prone to falling into a spirit of hurry?
• What tends to steal your peace or rush you through your days?

Read: Luke 5:15–16

- Even though people constantly needed Jesus' attention, what did He choose to do at the end of the passage?
- How might regular moments of quiet and prayer help you reconnect with God?
- How could a rhythm of stillness and rest positively affect your relationships?
- Who in your life might be blessed when you slow down and lead from a place of peace?

Reflect on this bold statement from Paul: "I urge you to imitate me." (1 Corinthians 4:16)

- Could you confidently say that to the people in your life? Why or why not?
- What would need to change in your daily walk with God for you to invite others to imitate your example?

Read: Luke 10:38–42 – the story of Mary and Martha

Mary stopped. She listened. She focused on Jesus. But how can we do this consistently in our day-to-day lives? How can we fix our eyes on Christ when everything around us feels urgent, chaotic, or overwhelming?

Sometimes it's in those very moments—when the pressure is rising and your energy is fading—that you need to pause and simply whisper a short prayer:
"God, be with me."
"God, give me the strength I need."

• Reflect on your past week:

Think back over the past few days or the past week. When were the moments you would have benefited from stopping? Were there times when slowing down—even briefly—might have protected your peace, helped you avoid anxious thoughts, or changed the way you responded?

Let's go deeper:
Eliminating hurry doesn't mean finishing more tasks—it means reordering your heart.
Scripture warns us against chasing distractions like:

Wealth

Approval

Image or recognition

Power

Worry over material needs

Comfort and pleasure

- Which of these worldly pursuits tend to distract you most?
- How do they contribute to feelings of hurry, restlessness, or anxiety?

Joy is a fruit of the Spirit.

When you walk in step with God, joy flows from within.

- On a scale of 1–10, how joyful are you right now?
- On a scale of 1–10, how joyful would others describe you as being? Is it the same? Why or why not?
- What steals your joy most often—worry, stress, hurry, comparison, or something else?

Accountability Check-In

(If pairing with the SoulStrength Fit workout program)

Workouts

- Were you able to complete your workouts this week?
- What helped you stay on track—or what made it challenging?
- How did you feel physically, mentally, or spiritually after completing your workouts?

Nutrition:

- How did you feel about your nutrition choices this week?
- What went well, and what do you feel good about?
- Were there any moments where it was tough to stay on track? What got in the way?

Daily Habits:

- Let's reflect on other daily habits—like hydration, protein intake, or sleep. Which of these went well for you this week?
- Were there any areas that felt especially challenging (e.g., drinking enough water, getting enough sleep, or planning meals ahead)?
- Did you notice yourself turning to food, snacks, or drinks for comfort or stress relief?
- What might help you respond differently next time?

Looking Ahead:

- What is one goal you want to focus on this coming week—whether it's a workout, a mindset shift, or a small habit to improve your health and alignment with God's design?

- How can the group support you and help you stay accountable?

Closing Prayer

Invite group members to share one thing they'd like prayer for—something personal, practical, or spiritual. Encourage them to reflect on the theme of slowing down and choosing joy. Close in prayer:

Lord, thank You for meeting us here. As we head into the week, help us slow down enough to notice You, listen to You, and find joy in Your presence. Give each of us the peace we need for the moments that feel rushed or overwhelming. Keep guiding our hearts back to You. Amen.

Week 3

Prayer & Confession

Spiritual Disciplines | Leader Guide – Week 3

Prayer & Confession

Opening Prayer

Lord, thank You for the chance to slow down and come before You. Help us be honest with You and with ourselves today. If we've been distracted, relying on ourselves, or holding onto things we should surrender, show us gently. Draw us into real conversation with You—help us talk to You openly, listen for Your voice, and trust You more deeply. Amen.

Discussion Questions

There are many reasons we may neglect prayer:

1. We often trust ourselves more than God and try to maintain control that was never ours.

2. Sometimes we doubt whether our prayers really matter—or if they're even heard.

3. Other times, we're simply too distracted to remember we've been invited into a limitless, personal conversation with the God of the universe.

   - Which of these three reasons do you most identify with?

- How has self-reliance, doubt, or distraction affected your prayer life?
- When have you felt your prayer life grow stronger or more intimate?

Read: Luke 9:23–24

- What does it mean to deny yourself and take up your cross?
- Give a few examples of how this might look in your daily life—your relationships, decisions, or priorities.
- Jesus calls us to surrender our own plans and desires. In what areas are you still holding on to control?
- Where might He be inviting you into deeper surrender?

Read: Matthew 6:7–8

"Do not be like them, for your Father knows what you need before you ask Him."

- How might your prayer life change if you deeply believed God already knows what you need—even before you ask?
- Would your prayers look different if your goal were to draw closer to God, not simply ask for things?
- Think about the focus of your usual prayers. What themes do you tend to repeat—comfort, gratitude, requests, praise?

Read: Luke 5:4–11

- Verse 11 tells us the disciples left everything and followed Him. What did they give up, and what might that have cost them?

- Following Jesus often comes with a cost—comfort, reputation, control, or worldly success.
- Can you think of a time that following Jesus cost you something? How did that experience shape your faith?

Read: 1 John 1:8–9

- How does God respond to those who confess their sins to Him?
- Many Christian thinkers have described the *Seven Deadly Sins*—pride, envy, anger, sloth, greed, gluttony, and lust. These often begin in our thoughts and attitudes before they ever show up in behavior.
- Which of these do you struggle with most?
- Can you trace any recurring actions or unhealthy patterns back to underlying thoughts or heart attitudes?

Accountability Check-In

(If pairing with the SoulStrength Fit workout program)

Workouts:

- Were you able to complete your workouts this week?
- What helped you stay on track—or what made it challenging?
- How did you feel physically, mentally, or spiritually after completing your workouts?

Nutrition:

- How did you feel about your nutrition choices this week?
- What went well, and what do you feel good about?

- Were there any moments where it was tough to stay on track? What got in the way?

Daily Habits:

- Let's reflect on other daily habits—like hydration, protein intake, or sleep. Which of these went well for you this week?
- Were there any areas that felt especially challenging (e.g., drinking enough water, getting enough sleep, or planning meals ahead)?
- Did you notice yourself turning to food, snacks, or drinks for comfort or stress relief? What might help you respond differently next time?

Looking Ahead:

- What is one goal you want to focus on this coming week—whether it's a workout, a mindset shift, or a small habit to improve your health and alignment with God's design?
- How can the group support you and help you stay accountable?

Closing Prayer

Invite group members to share one thing they'd like prayer for—something personal, practical, or spiritual. Close in prayer: Lord, thank You for hearing us and for welcoming us into Your presence just as we are. Help us walk into this week with open hearts—ready to pray, surrender, and trust You in both the small and big things. Draw us into deeper conversation with You each day. Amen.

Week 4

Training to be Like Christ

Spiritual Disciplines | Leader Guide – Week 4

Training to Be Like Christ

Opening Prayer

Lord, thank You for bringing us together. As we talk about what it looks like to grow and become more like You, help us be honest about the places where we feel stuck or unsure. Show us where You're inviting us to grow, and give us the courage to face those areas with You. Help us stay open, teachable, and willing to let You shape us. Amen.

Discussion Questions

Read: Ephesians 2:8–10

"For we are God's masterpiece..." (some translations say "handiwork")

God has created each of us with intention and purpose, but we often struggle to believe that.

- What keeps you from feeling like God's masterpiece most often? Is it unmet goals, comparison, or circumstances that didn't go as planned?
- When you struggle to believe you were created for good works, what is usually the root of that struggle?

Read: Psalm 1:3

"That person is like a tree planted by streams of water..."

- This verse paints a picture of a life deeply rooted in God—nourished, fruitful, and resilient.
- Which fruit of the Spirit (love, joy, peace, patience, kindness, goodness, faithfulness, gentleness, self-discipline) could you cultivate more by staying rooted in God's Word and presence?
- What rhythms help you remain planted near "streams of water" in your everyday life?

Read: John 15:1–2

"I am the true vine, and my Father is the gardener…"

Pruning is a necessary part of growth.

- Have you experienced a time when God was pruning something from your life?
- How did it feel, and how did you grow spiritually through that season?
- Is there anything in your life right now that God may be trying to prune—such as distractions, attitudes, or relationships?

Read: 2 Corinthians 10:5

"We take captive every thought to make it obedient to Christ."

Our spiritual formation includes renewing our minds.

- What thoughts about yourself, others, or life circumstances might you need to take captive?
- Are there recurring thoughts that need to be aligned more closely with the truth of God's Word?

- What Scripture might help you combat those thoughts?

Read: John 13:34–35

"Love one another. As I have loved you…"

Jesus calls us to love others as He has loved us—a command that requires the Holy Spirit.

- Are there people in your life who are hard to love?
- What situations bring out frustration, anger, or hurt in you?
- How can you invite God into those moments and relationships?
- Reflect on this truth: "You don't need to manufacture this love. Let Me love them through you."

Accountability Check-In

(If pairing with the SoulStrength Fit workout program)

Workouts:

- Were you able to complete your workouts this week?
- What helped you stay on track—or what made it challenging?
- How did you feel physically, mentally, or spiritually after completing your workouts?

Nutrition:

- How did you feel about your nutrition choices this week?
- What went well, and what do you feel good about?
- Were there any moments where it was tough to stay on track? What got in the way?

Daily Habits:

- Let's reflect on other daily habits—like hydration, protein intake, or sleep. Which of these went well for you this week?
- Were there any areas that felt especially challenging (e.g., drinking enough water, getting enough sleep, or planning meals ahead)?
- Did you notice yourself turning to food, snacks, or drinks for comfort or stress relief? What might help you respond differently next time?

Looking Ahead:

- What is one goal you want to focus on this coming week—whether it's a workout, a mindset shift, or a small habit to improve your health and alignment with God's design?
- How can the group support you and help you stay accountable?

Closing Prayer

Invite group members to share one thing they'd like prayer for—something personal, practical, or spiritual. Close in prayer:

Lord, thank You for the ways You're working in each of us. Help us stay rooted in You this week, notice where You're pruning, and allow You to renew our minds. Teach us to love others the way You've loved us, and keep leading us as we grow more like Christ. Amen.

Week 5

Humility, Servanthood, & Community

Spiritual Disciplines | Leader Guide – Week 5

Humility, Servanthood, & Community

Opening Prayer

Lord, thank You for bringing us together. As we talk about humility and what it looks like to serve like You, help us be honest about the places where pride or self-reliance creeps in. Show us where You're inviting us to grow, and give us the willingness to listen. Help us love one another well today and build real community rooted in grace. Amen.

Discussion Questions

Read: Philippians 2:3–4

"Do nothing out of selfish ambition or vain conceit. Rather, in humility value others above yourselves…"

This week's reading discusses how pride can show up in subtle yet powerful ways. Reflect on the list below. Are there any expressions of pride you've struggled with? Which resonates most with your current season of life?

Becoming overly concerned with your appearance or image; being preoccupied with how others perceive you

Considering yourself to always be right; valuing your opinion over others'

Rejecting correction or becoming defensive when confronted

Looking down on or excluding others rather than embracing them

Prioritizing your own needs over the needs of others

Reflection Questions:

When are you most tempted to slip into prideful thinking or behavior?

How does pride impact your relationships with others—or with God?

Humility: The Freedom to Be Real

Humility isn't about diminishing your worth or pretending to be less. It's the freedom to stop striving and simply accept who God made you to be. It's thinking of yourself less, not thinking less of yourself.

Consider this:

Would you benefit from being set free from any of the following?

Constant concern about what others think

Feeling criticized or defensive when corrected

A judgmental attitude or critical spirit toward others

The pressure to be special, impressive, or "better than" others

Which area stands out most for you today?

How might God be inviting you into greater humility and freedom?

Jesus and Servanthood

Jesus measured greatness in terms of service—not status. Reflect on the posture of your own heart when it comes to serving others.

Are you available to help even when it's inconvenient?

Do you become resentful when your plans or time are interrupted?

Are you willing to serve in small, simple, unseen ways?

Jesus washed feet, fed the hungry, and loved the outcast—no task was beneath Him. When or with whom is it most difficult for you to have a servant's heart?

Read: Matthew 5:1–12 – The Beatitudes

These statements from Jesus are deeply countercultural, inviting us to live in a way that shapes the world rather than conforming to it.

Which of the Beatitudes do you find most challenging or countercultural?

Is there one you struggle to believe or apply to your life?

Is there one you deeply resonate with right now?

How might you intentionally put one of these teachings into practice this week?

Serving in Secret

Serving without recognition is a powerful spiritual discipline. It frees us from the need to impress and roots our identity more deeply in God.

Ways to Serve Quietly This Week:

Do a household chore without being asked or acknowledged.

Make a drink or snack for someone as a quiet act of love.

Send an encouraging note anonymously.

Pray regularly for someone without telling them.

Make a quiet donation or perform an unseen act of kindness.

Reflection Questions:

How might you serve quietly this week?

What's one specific example of how you could intentionally love someone without seeking recognition?

How well do you receive acts of service from others?

Is it easy or difficult for you to accept help?

How might both giving and receiving help grow humility in your life?

Accountability Check-In

(If pairing with the SoulStrength Fit workout program)

Workouts:

- Were you able to complete your workouts this week?
- What helped you stay on track—or what made it challenging?
- How did you feel physically, mentally, or spiritually after completing your workouts?

Nutrition:

- How did you feel about your nutrition choices this week?

- What went well, and what do you feel good about?
- Were there any moments where it was tough to stay on track? What got in the way?

Daily Habits:

- Let's reflect on other daily habits—like hydration, protein intake, or sleep. Which of these went well for you this week?
- Were there any areas that felt especially challenging (e.g., drinking enough water, getting enough sleep, or planning meals ahead)?
- Did you notice yourself turning to food, snacks, or drinks for comfort or stress relief? What might help you respond differently next time?

Looking Ahead:

- What is one goal you want to focus on this coming week—whether it's a workout, a mindset shift, or a small habit to improve your health and alignment with God's design?
- How can the group support you and help you stay accountable?

Closing Prayer

Invite group members to share one thing they'd like prayer for—something personal, practical, or spiritual. Close in prayer: Lord, thank You for the example of Jesus—humble, gentle, and willing to serve in every way. Help us walk into this week with that same heart. Teach us to serve quietly, love freely, and build deeper community with one another. Keep shaping us into people who reflect You. Amen.

Week 6

Living for Christ

Spiritual Disciplines | Leader Guide – Week 6

Living for Christ

Opening Prayer

Lord, thank You for bringing us together. As we talk about what it means to live for You in our everyday lives, help us see where things feel out of balance or where we've been choosing comfort over growth. Show us the areas You're inviting us to trust You more deeply. Quiet our hearts so we can hear You clearly and follow You more closely. Amen.

Discussion Questions:

Many of us feel our schedules or priorities slipping out of control.

What currently feels out of balance in your life?

What would a more "balanced life" look like for you?

This week's devotional reminded us that while we often chase comfort, convenience, and manageability, God's priority is our growth.

Reflection:

Can you recall a time when God used discomfort, a trial, or a difficult season to grow your character or stretch your faith?

What did God teach you through that experience?

Guarding Your Heart

"Above all else, guard your heart,
for everything you do flows from it."
— Proverbs 4:23

When trials come, we face choices: to become bitter, discouraged, defeated… or to lean into God, trusting His refining work.

Reflection:

Considering a past or current trial, what does it mean for you personally to "guard your heart"?

How have you guarded your heart in difficult seasons—or how do you wish you had?

Comfort vs. Obedience

Sometimes we prioritize comfort even when God is calling us deeper.

In what area of your life do you tend to pursue comfort first?

What is one intentional step you could take this week to choose obedience, sacrifice, or spiritual growth instead?

How might you invite God to meet you in that uncomfortable space?

Positioning Your Heart to Hear God

True disciples don't just want God's truth—they position themselves to receive it through Scripture, prayer, solitude, and community.

Which habits or activities help you hear from God most clearly?

On the other hand, what habits or distractions most often prevent you from hearing Him?

When are you least likely to notice His voice or leading?

Read: Matthew 6:19–21

Where we direct our love, attention, and desire reveals the orientation of our hearts.

To cultivate a balanced heart, we must learn to love:

the right things

to the right degree

in the right way

with the right kind of love

Reflection:

Is there something in your life—wealth, work, beauty, talents, comfort, recognition—that you might love or pursue to the wrong extent?

On the flip side, is there something or someone
you're not loving enough, or not loving in the right way?

What stands out most as an area God may be realigning?

Living in the Name of Jesus

Colossians 3:17:

"Whatever you do, in word or deed, do everything in the name of the Lord Jesus..."

To act "in Jesus' name" means to live, respond, speak, and love in a way that reflects His character.

Consider everyday moments:

What would it look like to…

Wake up in Jesus' name?
What would your first thoughts be? What would you choose to focus on?

Work or manage your responsibilities in Jesus' name?
How would He approach your tasks, your pace, your attitude?

Love your family in Jesus' name?
How would He respond in moments of frustration, tension, or stress?

Handle driving, laundry, errands, or social media in Jesus' name?
How would He respond to rudeness, boredom, impatience, or unhelpful content?

Use your free time in Jesus' name?
What choices would reflect His priorities and His peace?

What is one specific area of your everyday life where you sense God calling you to increasingly live "in the name of Jesus"?

Accountability Check-In

(If pairing with the SoulStrength Fit workout program)

Workouts:

- Were you able to complete your workouts this week?
- What helped you stay on track—or what made it challenging?
- How did you feel physically, mentally, or spiritually after completing your workouts?

Nutrition:

- How did you feel about your nutrition choices this week?
- What went well, and what do you feel good about?
- Were there any moments where it was tough to stay on track? What got in the way?

Daily Habits:

- Let's reflect on other daily habits—like hydration, protein intake, or sleep. Which of these went well for you this week?
- Were there any areas that felt especially challenging (e.g., drinking enough water, getting enough sleep, or planning meals ahead)?
- Did you notice yourself turning to food, snacks, or drinks for comfort or stress relief? What might help you respond differently next time?

Looking Ahead:

- What is one goal you want to focus on this coming week—whether it's a workout, a mindset shift, or a small habit to improve your health and alignment with God's design?
- How can the group support you and help you stay accountable?

Closing Prayer

Invite group members to share one thing they'd like prayer for—something personal, practical, or spiritual. Close in prayer:

Lord, thank You for the ways You lead us. As we step into this week, help us live in a way that reflects You—in our thoughts, our choices, and our everyday routines. Give us wisdom to guard our hearts and strength to choose growth even when it's uncomfortable. Keep reminding us to do all things in Your name. Amen.

About the Author

Kelly Wenner is the founder and creator of SoulStrength Fit and SoulStrength Fit Kids. With more than two decades of experience in education, fitness, and faith formation, Kelly has devoted her life to helping others grow in their walk with the Lord through simple, daily habits that strengthen both body and spirit.

As a faith-based fitness expert and devotional author, Kelly is passionate about showing believers how to draw near to God in their everyday lives. Her mission is to inspire and equip others to cultivate spiritual disciplines—prayer, Scripture meditation, worship, and intentional living—that help them experience God's presence and follow Him more closely.

Spiritual Disciplines: Becoming More Like Christ reflects Kelly's heart for encouraging believers to connect with God in the small moments of each day and to pursue steady, faithful growth. These devotionals pair with her SoulStrength Fit faith-based fitness program, **Spiritual Disciplines**, which features at-home strength-training workouts designed to correspond with these devotionals—bringing time with the Lord into time spent strengthening your body.

Kelly lives in Southern California with her husband and daughters. She continues to find joy in serving others, writing devotionals, and creating programs that help people deepen their faith and live fully aligned with God's design.

To learn more, visit www.soulstrengthfit.com.

www.ingramcontent.com/pod-product-compliance
Lightning Source LLC
LaVergne TN
LVHW010950110826
845149LV00015B/3287

* 9 7 9 8 9 9 2 9 1 4 3 7 5 *